Delight by Design

A coloring book with guided reflections for discovering how to captivate your customers and create an Unstoppable Brand

Janet Wentworth

10X group

The 10X Group
Santa Rosa, California

Delight by Design: A coloring book with guided reflections for discovering how to captivate your customers and create an Unstoppable Brand

Published by:

The 10X Group

725 College Avenue, Suite 1

Santa Rosa, CA 95406

Email: janet.wentworth@gmail.com

www.unstoppablebrand.com

Unstoppable Brand™ of Janet Wentworth

First published in 2016

ISBN: 978-0-9895309-1-0

Printed in the United States of America

DISCLAIMER

This book is designed to provide small business owners with a process to discover their brand elements. The author and publisher make no representations or warranties and assume no liabilities of any kind with the respect to the accuracy or completeness of the content of this book or its suitability for any particular business. Unless otherwise specifically stated, the views are those of the author. Readers assume responsibility for their use of the information and ideas presented.

Preface

Delight by Design. What does this mean to you the small (or possibly solo) business owner?

Delighting your customers is your goal. Maybe you prefer charm, or captivate, or enchant. They all refer to an experience that provides great pleasure. Providing this delightful experience is the backbone of a successful business. People may buy once because you were the most convenient. Or the cheapest. Or you were running a Groupon deal. But if you want loyal customers. Ones who would pay more or go out of their way to patronize your business, you need to delight them.

So how do you delight people? There is no one quick answer to that question. Different populations will be delighted in different ways. People looking for an extreme sports coach are seeking a different experience than those looking for a relaxing spa treatment.

This is where the design comes in. You cannot leave creating a delightful experience to chance. Chance leads to inconsistency. One visit your customer is thrilled and the next time she feels neglected? that is a brand buster.

So you need a process to design your brand using a deep understanding of your Meaningful Few, the six brand drivers, and your vision for the business. Working this process is the way you design a brand and customer experience.

The good news even the smallest business with a tiny budget can do it. This isn't about money, it is about intentionally creating an experience and consistently delivering it.

So get your crayons out and take that first step to delighting your customers!

Contents

Introduction

Why Coloring Books?

Adult coloring books have become very popular, even earning a spot on the New York Times Best Seller list. They are popular as tools for stress relief, as an accessible creative outlet and for a nostalgia-driven activity. I became intrigued when I learned that coloring books not only relieved stress, but the act of coloring promoted focus, a positive mental state and creativity.

In the past people may have been embarrassed to be involved in a "children's" activity. Today people proudly show off their colored pages. Even more astounding, coloring has evolved from a solitary activity to a social one. Groups are now forming for group coloring events.

Obviously the coloring craze has legs. It fills an unmet need for reflection and creativity in our technology-crazed world. That is when it occurred to me that there was an application for coloring books in marketing and branding.

Why a Branding Coloring Book?

When I talk to my clients about branding, I get one of two responses: "I haven't thought about it" or "I have a logo and a package design." End of story. If I push for a more, I get very superficial responses.

But branding is so important. It can't be left to chance any more than following the "build it and they will come" mantra will create a successful business. More importantly, branding is so valuable for a small business owner struggling to do all that they need to do while dealing with the overwhelm of creating and running a business and the usual shortfall of cash.

A strong, intentionally nurtured brand is magic for a small business. So how do you get people to take the time for considered reflection about their brand? Enter the coloring book!

The coloring book with questions for you to ponder as you color is the perfect way to get your distracted brain to focus on your brand elements. Coloring will help you uncover ideas that you would never have realized while making a list or building a spreadsheet. These ideas need quiet time to bubble to the surface. They need a free mind to create connections you had not thought of.

Intentionally reflective coloring can be the way for you to discover how to delight your customers. Delight is the feeling you want to create. But it is such a fuzzy concept. Exactly how do you delight customers? How do you get your hands around this idea of delight to create specific, concrete and repeatable actions to build a tribe of your raving fans?

Well, it isn't as difficult as you may think. It also doesn't require a big budget. You already understand (and may already have) a logo, company colors, a web site, business cards, a flyer. Why not start with those and build from there? And as long as you are designing these visual pieces of your brand, why not design the non-visual elements of your brand with intention? It won't cost any more.

This book is not meant as a quick fix. It is meant to encourage you to reflect on what you are trying to build. Don't shortchange the process. Sit back. Breathe. Enjoy. And design the business you desire.

HOW TO USE THIS BOOK. The book is written is a specific order but skip around if you like. Go with the inspiration that comes to you.

Each section has four pages:
1. Explanation of the topic.
2. Questions for guided reflection. Use the reflections as a starting point, but think up your own questions as well.
3. Page for you to color.
4. Blank page for your thoughts. This last page is for written ideas, possibly a mindmap, or even clippings from a magazine or web sites. This is your page to use as you like to record your ideas. Or maybe you will use a separate piece of paper to record random thoughts as you color and use this page to record those ideas you want to implement. Take your choice. Be open to possibilities.

Start where you are.
Use what you have.
Do what you can.

Arthur Ashe

Vision

What is your vision for your business? There is no one simple answer. You may be creating a part time business that will bring in needed income, it might be a full-time one-person operation. It might be something you see growing to include several employees. It might be a hobby business where you sell on Etsy. Maybe you see an office, a restaurant, a store front or light manufacturing plant in your future. You might want outlets in several cities. Maybe you dream of franchising it in the future.

These are all viable visions. Don't let anyone talk you out of your dream because they think you can't pull it off. It is your dream. Go for it!

You know the regular advice: Start with the end in mind. This works for vacation planning as well as starting a business. If you have franchising in mind, maintaining records of what you do that works, your systems, and your processes will make it much easier to create a franchise-able business.

If you want a business that fits with your life—be it children in school, a parent you are caregiver for, or your many unrelated hobbies, plan ahead for how this will work. Make sure your dream business is a viable business and one that fits with the other parts of your life.

Do you plan to hire employees? Have you thought about how to inspire them? Of perhaps you plan to find online resources such as web developers, graphic designers and virtual assistants. Do you know how you will easily convey your brand to them so they can work efficiently and deliver what you want?

Are you bootstrapping this business, doing everything yourself and learning as you go? Fine. The clearer your vision, the easier it will be to maximize your efforts and avoid getting overwhelmed. Or distracted by all the great things you could do . . . but just don't have the bandwidth for right now.

So what does your future business look like?

Reflections on Your Vision

- Think about how you already picture this business. Rethink each element. Is it still valid? Is it important? Why is it important to you?

- What is your business uniqueness? What should people choose you over other solutions or ways to spend their money?

- What are your key products and/or services?

- What shape will it take? Physical presence? Online? Service delivered at client site? Or?

- Who is your competition? What advantages do they have? Is doing nothing an option for them? Or might they be do-it-yourselfers?

- The self-made man/woman is largely a myth. There are always influencers, partners, referral agents, supporters, angels in the background. Who can you call on?

- What are your assets? Not just physical assets, like money, delivery van, etc. What about skills? Past experiences? Name recognition in your industry? Connections? Social media following? Or?

- What do you want people to think about your business? What is the feeling you are trying to generate? There will be one reflection on this later, but it is good to start with this desired feeling.

- What are your budget constraints? How will this influence what you are able to do? Do you have workarounds or creative approaches to mitigate the lack of funding?

- What is your positioning in your market? Are you the Costco or the Tiffany? Are you the Walmart or the neighborhood pharmacist? Are you the generic outlet or the custom option?

What Is Your Vision?

Why Me?

How much thought have you given to why you are the right person for this business?

We often start a business because we have a passion for something or we feel we are good at something. An IT worker who gets laid off, may start a freelance IT consulting practice. Or you are a dyed-in-the-wool crafter and think there is a market for your creations. Nothing wrong with that.

But if you want a strong brand for your business you need to dig a bit deeper.

This is the personal side of why someone should choose your company. People will choose you if what you offer is better, if they love the experience, if you are cheaper, or for one of many other reasons. That is the external answer to the question of why people should buy from you.

But the internal question must also be answered. Why should you do this? Why does the market need you? Why are you so passionate about this that you will overcome the obstacles and demonstrate the grit needed to the stay the course? Starting a business is always harder than we think it will be. It also takes longer to be a success.

So many people start a business and expect almost instant success. They want to be profitable in three months. It rarely works like that. More likely there are many lean months before the business gains traction and builds a following. You might have to modify your offering based on customer input. You might even need to completely reinvent your business model.

What will keep you going during the dark days is an unwavering belief in what you are doing. You truly believe there is an audience clamoring for what you offer. And you believe in yourself as the one who can do this. The one who must do this.

It is this belief that gets you up every morning to fight the good fight for your business.

Ask yourself again, why you?

Reflections on Why Me?

- Why are you starting this business? Give the truth. It is OK to start a business because you need the money. Maybe you were laid off and need to keep working. Maybe you retired and decided you didn't like it. Maybe an unexpected need came up, like a family medical emergency, and you just need the money. Any of these is a reasonable response. Just don't feel you need some high-minded reason that isn't authentic.

- Even if you are in it only for the money, there must be some reason you chose this specific business. What appealed to you? Something you already know how to do? Something you have always wanted to try? Something you feel needs doing?

- Is there a natural connection with your intended customers? You love to knit so you are opening a yarn store? You have spent years traveling and now want to do personally guided tours? If you have no interest in interior decorating and decide to buy a window covering franchise, this could be a problem as you have little to offer your customers. What do you have to offer?

- Why do you think you will be able to make this business work? What about you, your dreams, your skills, your experience, and your personal habits will give you the grit to keep going?

- Do you believe that people need, really need, what you offer? That your service is unique? That the need will go unfilled without you?

- Have you ever worked with someone you think is the perfect customer? Can you write a simple story of how your service or product helped this person? Having a story like this is the perfect antidote to feeling like giving up (which is very common at some point in a business life). People can achieve the most wondrous results when they have a story of why they need to keep going.

- If you are having trouble coming up with answers, why not talk to a friend and get a fresh perspective.

WHY ME?

Why Are You the One?

Meaningful Few

Meaningful Few may be a new term for you. The usual way to describe the customers you seek is target customer (or target audience).

The idea of a target customer is from the 1980's and the marketing-as-war mindset. It was quite popular thanks to the book Marketing Warfare by Al Ries and Jack Trout. The subtitle is "How American corporations are using military strategies to outmaneuver, outflank and even ambush their competition!" If the subtitle isn't enough to get the message across, the cover has small tanks coming out of a briefcase to complete the visual.

I have yet to meet a small business owner or solopreneur who could warm up to the marketing-as-war philosophy.

These people are starting a business from a personal passion. An inner drive to do something good and yet still make money. They care about their customers and are willing to slog through the dark days of starting a business because of an inner fire.

Mostly, they are very open and welcoming. They see opportunities and look for partnerships.

The marketing-warfare types see a zero sum game: a dollar spent with a competitor is one dollar less for me.

When writing a marketing plan, writing about the Target Customer is uncomfortable.

Enter the Meaningful Few. The term comes from the Pareto principle or, as it is commonly known. the 80/20 rule. Eighty percent of your sales will come from twenty percent of your customers. Those twenty percent are the Meaningful Few. The other eighty percent are the trivial many. Thinking of your best customer as Meaningful opens up all sorts of possibilities. Why are they meaningful to you? But also, why are you meaningful to them?

Reflections on Your Meaningful Few

- If you already have a business, who are your best customers? The ones you wish you could clone?

- What makes them your best customers? Why do you like working with them?

- What defines these people? Demographics, like age, income levels, education, political or religious affiliation, etc.?

- Move on to the behaviors that define them. Where do they live? What kind of car do they drive? How do they dress? Where do they vacation? What wine club do they belong to or golf course do they play? What is their favorite restaurant?

- Where else do they shop? Are they Window users or Apple fans? Do they support Kickstarter projects? Do they buy at Walmart, the local grocer or have groceries delivered?

- Each of these behaviors gives insights into the character of the person. Pretend you are Sherlock Holmes. Envision one of your best customers (or a hoped for customer, if you are just starting out). What can you deduce from their appearance and behaviors?

- What do they want their life to look like? How would they change their life if they could? Live in a better neighborhood? Go back to school? Find a more fulfilling job? Learn to play the tuba?

- Why is your business important to them? How do you fit in this vision for a better life?

- How does the picture you have painted of your Meaningful Few illustrate why they are great customers for your business? In the why of each personal characteristic are the answers to what you need to do to nurture a brand that will appeal to him/her. The whys will illustrate shared values. The whys will show where you can connect and delight them.

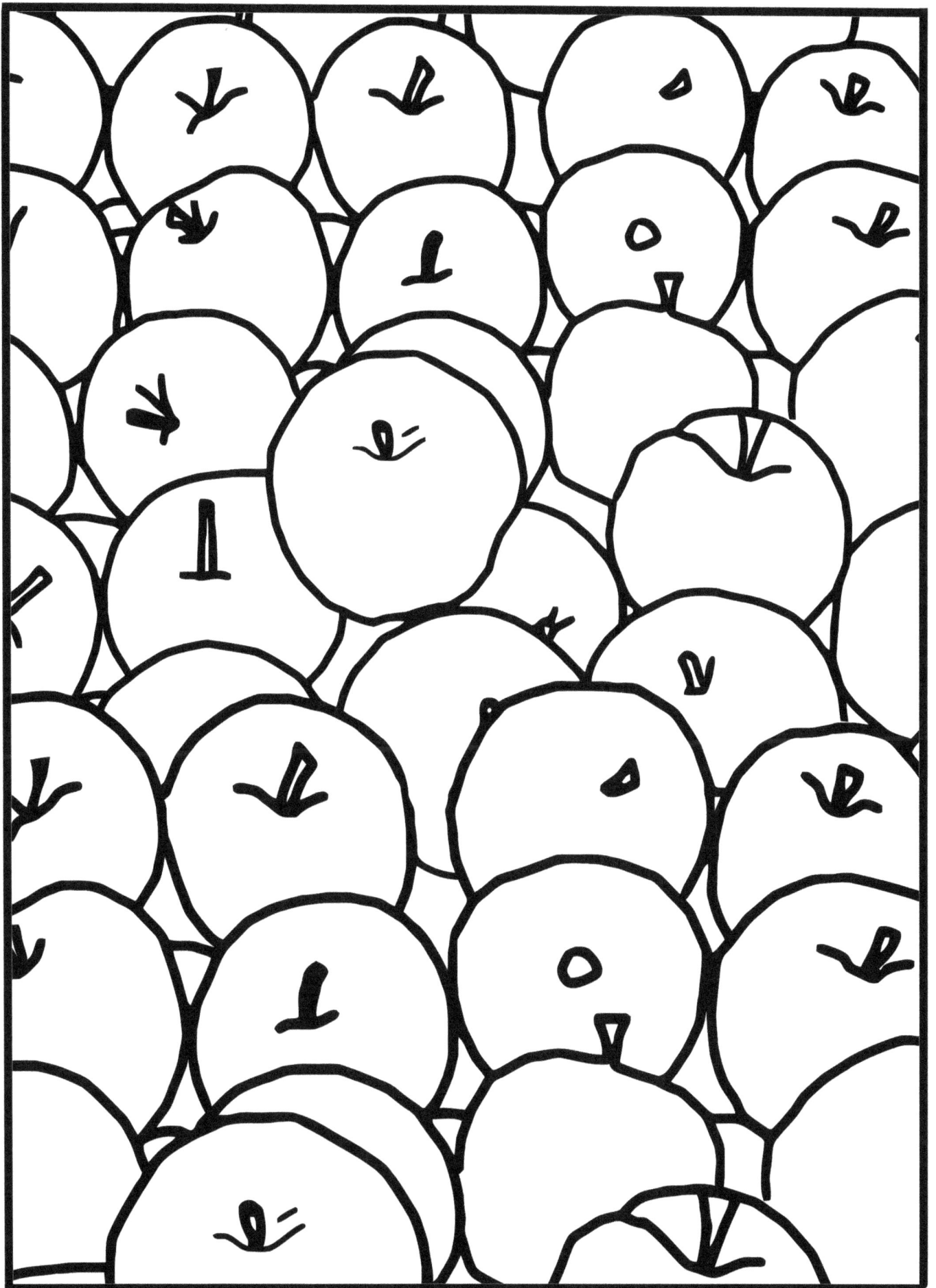

Who Are Your Meaningful Few?

Feeling

"I've learned that people will forget what you said, people will forget what you did, but people will never forget how you made them feel." Maya Angelou

Maya Angelou is not remembered as a great marketer, but she clearly understands what a brand is. It isn't your logo or tag line. It isn't some evil plot to manipulate consumers. It isn't only for large consumer products. And it isn't something to be avoided because, well you are just too darn overwhelmed with everything else you need to do to even thinking about branding.

This is all wrong-headed. Every business has a brand. In fact, every person has a brand.

A brand is what a person thinks when they hear your name (where "your" can be you or your business). Notice I didn't say when "people" hear your name. Brand is personal.

Some people love Trader Joe's markets. They find them exciting, full of quirky, exotic food products, happy employees and a great escape from the usual bland grocery store. But others find Trader Joe's annoying. From its rather eclectic mix of products to its usually cramped parking lots, visiting TJ's is an experience of fearing for your car's safety and leaving empty handed because you couldn't find the "regular stuff" that you needed. Then there are those who think "meh" when they hear the TJ name.

Each person is correct. And your job as a business owner is to understand your best customers, what delights them and offer them that experience in spades. You can never make everyone happy, so why try? Instead double down on the ones who share your values, love what you offer, and are delighted by the experience.

What is the feeling you want people to have at the sound of your name?

Reflections on Desired Feeling

- You might start this exercise by thinking about other brands you love. What do you feel about them? Why do you love them?

- Think terms of single words, like comfortable, or longer phrases, like "they are always so appreciative when I come in."

- Now think of your own business. What would you love them to think about you? Write down as many ideas as you can think of.

- Think about your competition. Competition may be less obvious than you think. If you are a movie house, people might stay home with Netflix. If you are a restaurant, people may eat in (or at a cheaper place) to save for a kitchen remodel. The option of doing nothing is also competition. As is the option to do-it-yourself.

- Review the feelings you identified. Are they strong enough to get people to buy? Or is the competition more attractive? Is doing nothing is a serious option?

- How do the feelings you identified fit with your view of your Meaningful View? Does it relieve the pain? Does it make them happy? Happy enough to buy? And become loyal customers?

- What specifically will make them come back? Or will it be a one-off sale? Why are the feelings you generate so powerful for them?

- You may have several categories of Meaningful Few. Many business do. Will these feelings you have identified work for all of them? If not, do you need special branding elements for some categories.

- Are you thinking of all the possibilities? Or are you thinking of things you can do? Don't restrict your thinking at this point. Don't discard idea with a flip "I could never do that." Think big. Be audacious. You never know when you can find an alternate path to that audacious goal.

How Will You Make People Feel?

Happiness

Traditional marketing plans include a problem/solution section. The concept is that if you can identify a prospect's pain you can position your product/service as the solution. Is it easier to sell someone your dental services when their tooth is throbbing than when they are feeling great.

Understanding your customer's problem and how you will solve it can be important. The thought process gets you out of features and benefits and into solving the real pain that will move them to buy.

But I have found the pain/solution process can be limiting. It puts you in a box. Identify the pain, solve the problem, get the sale. It focuses on the negative, even though your solution offers a positive resolution.

A more useful (rewarding and profitable) perspective is to get out of that box by expanding your thinking to what will make your customers happy.

What makes you happy when you are thinking about some of your favorite businesses. It might be the dentist who has funny pictures pasted on the ceiling for you to look at while in the chair. Maybe it is a child's play area in the clothing store or treats for your dog. Perhaps it is abandoning those canned scripts for customer service reps and just letting them talk to the caller, person to person.

Think of how your branding elements can include something "happy." This isn't a sappy "think happy" reflection. It is a mindset that gets you thinking beyond the basics of satisfying the basic need and into the wide open space of possibilities.

People are attracted to the small things. Those unexpected treats that catch us by surprise and make us smile.

What can you do to make your customers smile?

Reflection on Creating Happiness

- Imagine one person who represents your Meaningful Few. Think of the buying process for what you offer. Where along the way can you add a bit of unexpected happiness?

- Does your customer shop with a spouse? A child? A pet? Can you do something for these companions to support a better shopping experience for your customer?

- What is related to what you sell but normally part of the sale?

- The following five ways to make buying a happier event are from the book Happy Money: The Science of Happier Spending by Elizabeth Dunn & Michael Norton. Flip them around to see if as a seller you can make it a happier buying process for your customer.

- **Sell an experience.** This is especially true if the experience includes others. Are there ways for you to create an experience (alone or with others) from what you sell?

- **Make it a Treat.** We enjoy things (be it a fabulous vacation or a bowl of M&Ms) when they are not always available. When we can enjoy the anticipation. Limited time offers, once a year sales, cherry pie on the menu only one month a year. The limited availability will make your product more desirable. What can you make a treat?

- **Sell Time.** Some people find vacuuming meditative. Others just go out and buy a Roomba. Getting more free time only brings happiness when you do something that makes you happy with those hours. Selling time is easier if your business is an obvious fit, like a lawn mowing service. Do you have a creative way to give your customizers the feeling of more time?

- **Sell Now Enjoy Later.** Do you remember the layaway plan? Who wants to go on vacation and pay for it later when the tan has faded. How can your customers pay in advance and enjoy later?

- **Encourage Investing in Others.** Spending money on others makes us happier than spending on ourselves. Can you offer scholarships A discount if someone buys two and gives one to someone in need? Instead of a company donation, how can you involve the customer in the contribution?

How Will You Make Them Happy?

Beliefs

If you have ever created a business plan you are familiar with the section for company values. We are professional. Or competent. Or customer-focused. We have integrity. Or passion. Wegmans grocery chain uses Caring, High Standards, Making a Difference, Respect, Empowerment.

At first glance they sound good, but what do any of these words mean? How would you see it in action? Will this value to help in your business decisions? Probably not. They are too vague, ill-used, abused.

Asking people what they believe gets a more thoughtful and useful response. To describe your belief, you have to make a full statement. That usually results in specifics and details. A belief shows a vision for a better future. We can recognize a belief in action.

Here are two belief statements.

Warby Parker: We believe that buying glasses should be easy and fun. It should leave you happy and good-looking, with money in your pocket.

Dave's Killer Bread We believe everyone is capable of greatness. We believe in the power of reinvention, and are committed to turning second chances into lasting change.

Notice how these belief statements include the customer. They want customers to have good vision, to have fun, get a second chance.

By opening up their beliefs they attract people who also have those values. You want beliefs that will attract your Meaningful Few. Belief statements help us see the better world this company is contributing to. And we want to be in that world as well.

A final thought: a belief is not a slogan. Your slogan may come from thinking about your beliefs but don't get caught up in trying to make a catchy tag line. Your values are the serious underpinning of your business.

Reflections on Your Beliefs

- What are your beliefs?

- Use the 5 Whys process to get at your core beliefs. The 5 Whys process starts with your first thought. Then you ask yourself "Why is this important?" to uncover a deeper thought and continue digging down through the layers until you are at the root belief. Use ideas from your Vision and Why Me? exercises as a springboard for identifying your beliefs.

- What personal values/beliefs do you have that you bring to this business?

- Where do profits fit in your business plan?

- How will you treat your customers?

- Do you have other businesses you want to use as a model for yours?

- Do you have beliefs that bring happiness? Don't get stuck in the rut of thinking beliefs must all be serious and high-minded. Beliefs that bring joy are important.

- Do you have beliefs around the way you deliver your service or product?

- Do you have beliefs around how your treat your employees?

- Are your belief statements "we are" or "we want to be"? Avoid the aspirational "want" statements. They can be a slippery slope of good intentions but not reality.

- Do you have any stories / anecdotes that show these beliefs in action? If you have had to make a tough decision because your belief clashed with the easy solution, you know if the belief is true or not.

Beliefs

What Are Your Beliefs?

Look

How you look is one of the most utilized drivers of any company's brand. No surprise here as humans are very visual creatures. But how much thought have you given to your entire appearance? Did you decide on some colors and a logo and think you are done?

How you look includes your signage, your packaging, your store front, your web site, your business cards, your invoices, your emails, your display racks, your employee uniforms, maybe even your hair style or tattoos. The list goes on.

Everything someone sees that represents you needs to be intentionally created and consistent.

If you are a solo business, how you dress becomes part of your brand. Sonia Simone of Copyblogger calls herself the Pink Haired Marketer. Of course she is easy to spot with her pink-streaked hair. My local Oliver's grocery store has a cheese monger sporting a giant Mohawk. At well over a foot high it is hard to miss. For Bastille Day he decorated it with French flags and historical images and quotations creating a virtual French history lesson in his hair.

A little too far out for you? It's OK to be subtle. It's not OK to be random. It's not OK for your appearance to be a mis-match with your brand in the eyes of your Meaningful Few.

All of these visual pieces become your style. And your style should remain consistent so people will recognize you. You can tell an Apple ad from a Harley ad without any logos present. They have two completely different styles.

How you look can offer opportunities for very low cost branding. You may already have personal attributes that can work here, even if you don't have a 12inch high Mohawk. Make the most of it.

Reflections on How You Look

- Do you have a logo that works for the brand you want? Why is it right for your brand?

- Do you have a primary color, secondary color and one or two accent colors you use consistently?

- Is your web site a reflection of the brand you want? Or was it done with a generic theme and little customization that would make it distinctively yours? Are there ways you can make it more distinctive and true to your brand?

- How do your print pieces look? Are they consistent with your brand visual assets (logo, color, design aesthetic) or are they a hodge-podge? How could you make the branding stronger? Are you using low coast design services that are hindering your brand? Penny wise and pound foolish?

- Do your social spaces reflect your brand look? Do you use the same avatar consistently?

- What about your signage? Even the little signs. Most people get the big stuff right, but often stumble on the details.

- Do you use uniforms for your staff? How do they fit in as a brand device? Are you like Henneke Duistermaat, the copywriter. Her brand colors are orange and purple and she is always seen in her videos wearing a purple wrap blouse.

- How about tattoos? Possibly earrings or other jewelry that is distinctive and reflects your brand?

- Do you have a company mascot? A mascot may not be appropriate for all businesses but might be useful. Henneke uses a hand-drawn cartoon of her sidekick Henrietta for all of her blog posts for a unique look. She actually took a cartoon class so she could develop this mascot on her own!

- Do you use visual props? I had a client whose business was helping people deal with self-defeating habits. She carried a can of WD-40 with her to illustrate her job of helping people get unstuck.

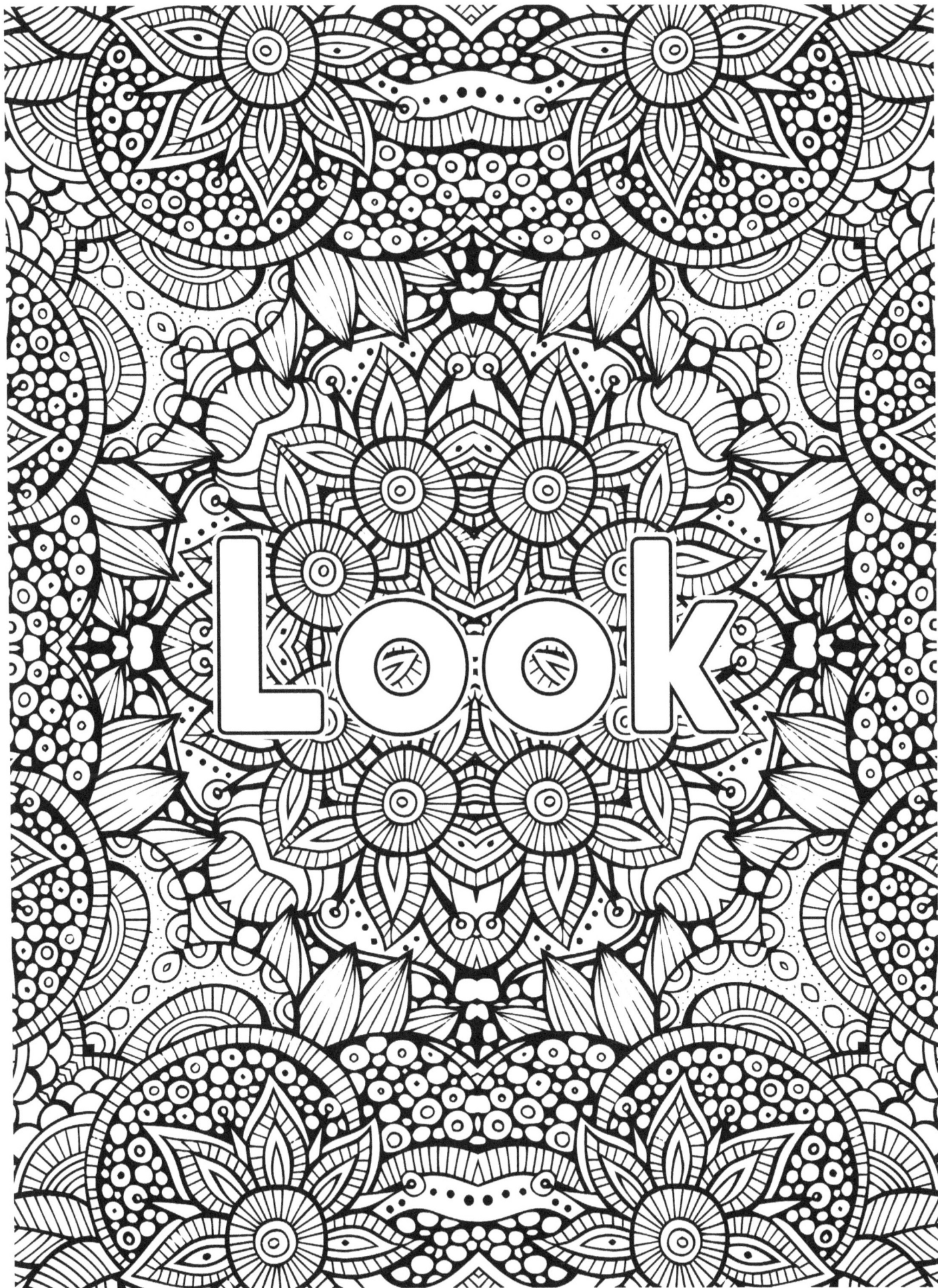

How Will You Look?

Say

What you say covers more than you might think.

First there is the tone of voice. Are you soft and comforting? Or a tough as nails drill sergeant barking out orders? One isn't better than the other. They are just different and you need to find the tone of voice that works for your Meaningful Few. Do you use a lot of slang? Swear words? Possibly even brutal language. But it doesn't work for everyone. Unsure of your tone?

What are your sacred words? Are there words that are used in your industry? Over and out. FIFO. Social graph. SEO. Businesses frequently have insider words that their loyal fans know. Starbucks Venti vs Grande. Apple's Genius Bar. Your tag line falls in the sacred words category.

Watch what you write and what you say and notice when certain words and phrases are repeatedly used. These are sacred words, as long as they are used intentionally.

Do you have useful metaphors or comparisons? Are you the Uber of lawnmowers or the Nespresso of kale smoothies?

What is your writing style? Do you write short sentences? Crisp language is your hallmark? Or maybe you have a more academic style. Long sentences. Lots of Oxford commas. Maybe even the dreaded passive voice. If it is right for your audience, fine. Just be consistent.

Product Names Product/service names are sacred words as well. They should be unique to you and extend your brand personality. We know Apple products by the ever-expanding list of iProducts. Harley Davidson uses words like FatBoy, and Road King. How do your product names stack up? Are they clearly identifiable to you or are they more generic?

Reflections on What You Say

- Have you already selected sacred words? Were they chosen intentionally or was it unintentional?

- Why are these words meaningful to your customers?

- How do these words create a sense of belonging?

- What makes them important to your brand?

- Do you have a list of these words so everyone knows how to use them?

- What is your writing style? Is this the one your Meaningful Few will love?

- Do multiple people write for your web site? Or you use hired writers for brochures or blog posts? Do they share your style? Can you explain your style to them?

- Do you have metaphors to help explain concepts or make product benefits easier to grasp?

- How do you choose your product names? Are they reflective of your company personality? Do you dig deep to find just the right names or go with generic names like gold, silver and bronze membership levels?

- Where can you add sacred words?

    - phone greetings

    - title of your blog

    - personal greeting

    - email signature

    - your slogan

    - other places?

What Will You Say?

Do

Specifically, what you do to delight your customers?

You have already defined your Meaningful Few and what will delight them, right? So now I want you to expand on that with the specific, repeatable, intentional things you will be doing to make this happen.

Do you remember the JC Penny branding debacle? They brought Ron Johnson from Apple to be the new CEO. Apparently he didn't realize that JC Penny customers were not like Apple customers. They are people on fixed budgets. People who have the option of buying similar clothes, shoes, etc. at other stores. People who were loyal to Penny's for the confusing array of coupons and specials! They loved the thrill of the hunt and scoring a bargain.

Johnson thought he was making the system better for his customers. Instead he was taking away their reason for buying. Customers left in droves. Revenues dropped 51%. Ron Johnson lost his job.

This is a great lesson is doing what your customers want, not what you think is good for them.

But, "doing" is more than coupons and promotions. Doing can be how you treat people (here it overlaps with what you say and with rituals). It can be special services you offer, like delivery or special orders or custom services. It can be the fact that you offer packages of services with specific benefits rather than sell your service by the hour. Or that you have a customer loyalty program. Or offer referral bonuses.

Or perhaps it is your social consciousness. You support a local non-profit. You follow the Tom's one-for-one model. You use your values, be it frugal shopping or save the planet, to inform what you offer and how you offer it.

Reflections on What You Do

- Reflect back on your values. Just having values is not enough. How do they inform what you do?

- Reflect on your Meaningful Few. How does your understanding of them inform what you do, what you offer and how you offer it?

- Do you have a system for adding new products / services? Does it include alignment with your values, Your Meaningful Few and your desired brand? Can you make this linkage stronger?

- What do you do that is different from the competition? Are you a copycat or an innovator when it comes to what you offer and how you create your customer experience?

- You probably already have the basics covered, so what sort of surprises can you add to the mix? Free treats in the store? Unexpected free samples in the bag? Thank you gifts for a great referral? Some activities can be rituals and others can be surprises. Do you have both?

- In seeking new ideas do you involve your customers, such as with a customer advisory board?

- Do you ever use surveys to get a deeper understanding of your customers and help you uncover new things to do for them?

- Do you offer coupons? Promotions? Joint marketing with other related businesses? Bring-a-friend nights? Support for a local non-profit?

- What you do covers the big actions as well as tiny ones. Just as a cinematographer uses close-ups and panoramic views, use variety to keep it interesting.

- Can you do mock customer interactions to see where you might find new ways to delight your customer?

Do

What Will You Do?

Senses

You might think this is an optional brand driver. If you are a spa owner, sensory elements will be a natural part of your branding. Fragrant candles burning. Hot herbal teas waiting. The soothing texture of body creams. Warm snuggly robes. Calming pictures on the wall. You have all the bases covered.

But what if you have an IT installation business? Not so easy to think of sensory elements here.

Sensory elements are so tied up in memories they are worth seeking for your business. You probably won't be able to use them all and may not even want to. Perhaps one or two perfect sensory elements are all you need. Let them stand out rather than being part of a noisy sensory experience.

The sensory elements you need to think about are:

- **Sounds.** Think bells ringing. Jingles. Music. Audible alerts. The sound of a computer booting up. Old fashioned cash registers. McDonalds' I'm Lovin' It tune.

- **Fragrance.** Think beyond obvious perfumes or outdoor fragrances. What about that new car smell? Or the fresh cut wood scent of a new fence being built? A Cinnabon in the mall, anyone?

- **Taste.** This is easy if you have an ice cream shop. You can offer the flavor of the day. Or have a signature flavor. But if you are a financial advisor, what about a bowl of unusual peppermints sitting out for every client meeting? Send chocolate chip cookies to clients on their birthdays?

- **Texture.** Easy if you are a fabric store. Or a furrier. Harder if you are an online business. Perhaps though it can be in your packaging. A jewelry store may use velvet or silk pouches. A local shoe store may wrap the shoe boxes in rough twine.

Take your time with sensory branding. The best ideas may not be obvious.

Reflections On Sensory Elements

- You may think yourself lucky if you have an obvious sensory element to use. But you may want to reconsider. The obvious elements are probably used by others in your industry. Does yours stand out? Or do you use gardenia candles and they use rose and you think this is good enough?

- It is better to think about ways to make your signature sensory elements unique. And surprising. Unexpected. And relevant. This isn't a race to create the greatest number of sensory elements. A few signature, memorable elements will be far more powerful than a hodgepodge of so-so ideas.

- Once you have some in place, they become agents of anticipation for your customers and begin to work their magic. How are your sensory elements creating anticipation?

- **Sounds.** Think of sounds for your business. Your doorbell. Your telephone ring tone. Any machinery noises. Opening boxes, jars, car doors or? What about a jingle you use in ads? Or maybe you are a singer or play a musical instrument? Do you have music playing in your shop? Jazz? Reggae? Hip Hop?

- **Fragrance.** Fragrances are easy to overuse. And easy to just take the first one that comes to mind. Evaluate any fragrance ideas you have. Are they common or a real signature for your business? Avoid the so-so ideas. Go for the standouts.

- **Taste.** You may never have thought of taste for your business. You are an accountant or a business consultant. Or maybe a plumber. But don't give up so easily. I am known for my homemade English toffee at Christmas. Packaged in white boxes, with red ribbons, it is anticipated and missed if I go on vacation around Christmas and miss a delivery!

- **Texture.** Think about your packaging. Any chance for a memorable texture here? Or in your bags? What about tactile business cards? A signature texture might be elusive, but don't give up. Let the idea percolate. You never know when a great idea might strike!

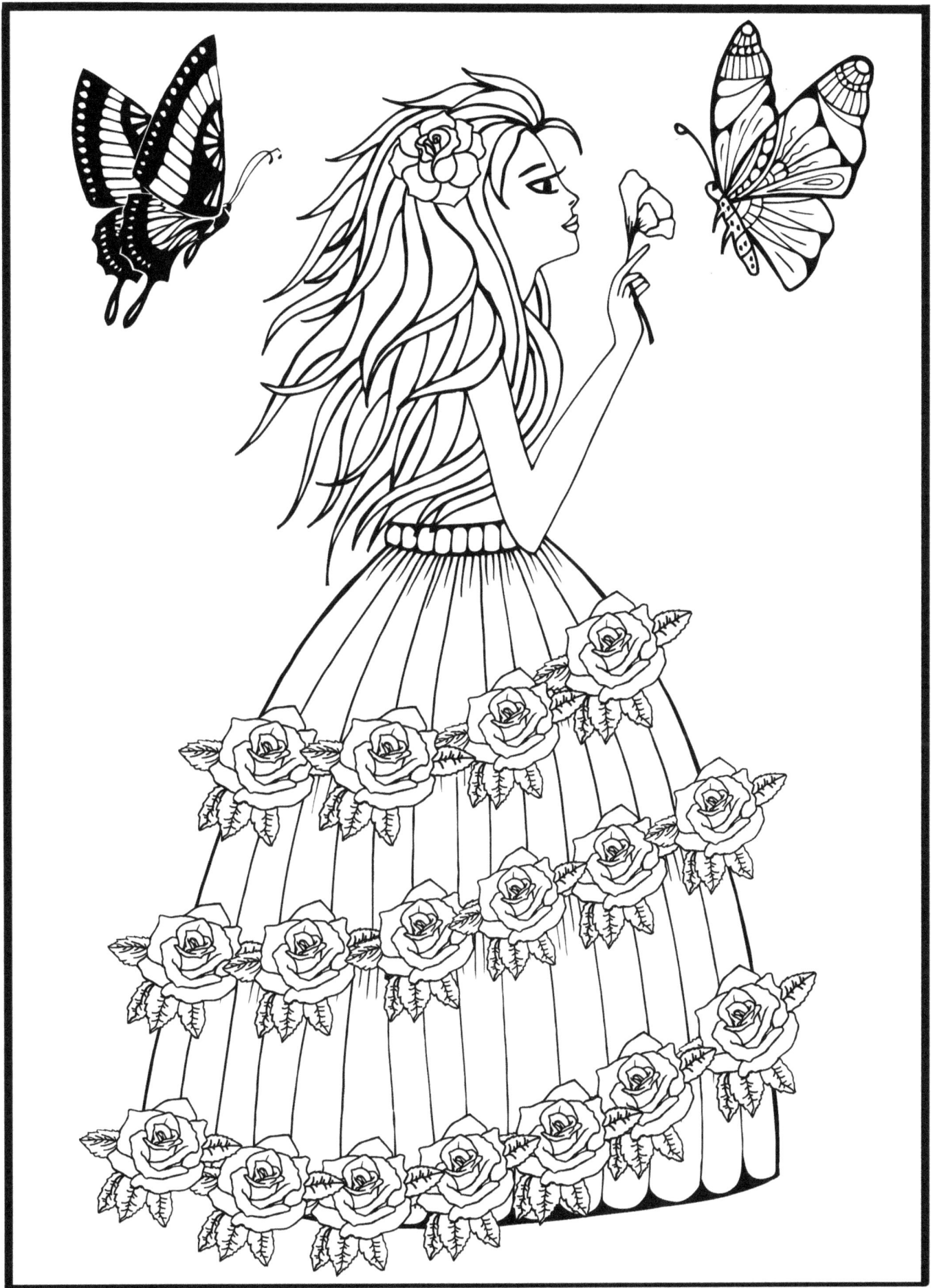

What Are Your Sensory Ideas?

Rituals

Rituals are the unsung hero of branding. Mention branding and people will automatically reply "logo." In over 10 years of business advising and workshops I have never had a person blurt out, "rituals!" What a shame, as rituals are such a powerful driver for your brand.

What is a ritual? It is a repeated action. It can be a ceremony, like a marriage or graduation. Or it can be going to the dentist for your annual cleaning and exam. In all these cases you know what to expect. Taking your daughter to a parking lot to practice before a driver's license exam. These are the big rituals of our lives. But there are little rituals as well.

How you make your coffee in the morning. Brushing your teeth. The order you put on your clothes. The checklist you use before leaving home on vacation. Because these are automatic, we don't think of them as rituals.

Businesses have opportunities for rituals as well. How you greet customers. The experience they have in your store or in your workshop. How you set up an appointment for installation. Your follow-up after the work is done. All of these, if done intentionally and consistently, can become valuable rituals for your customers.

Rituals can also be done by customers with your products or services. Unpacking your product can be a ritual. Have you designed it to be enjoyable or do you just stuff the product in a bag? Some products, say tea, lend themselves to rituals in the way the tea is brewed or even that the customer saves the tea for special occasions. These rituals that happen out of your sight can be very powerful.

Intentionally setting the stage for these ritual opportunities will strengthen the bond of the customer with your business. What can you do to nurture these rituals?

Reflections on Your Rituals

- Think about your favorite companies. What rituals do they have? Why do you like them? Are there any you wish they would create?

- What rituals do you already have in place? Walk through the entire new customer process and see where there are opportunities for rituals. Walk through the process for repeat customers. And again for unhappy customers. Be especially attuned to the little opportunities for ritual.

- Every touch point with a customer is an opportunity. You may not be physically present for there to be a ritual. Opening your email newsletter. Visiting your web site. Listening to your podcast. How can you turn these routine marketing efforts into a ritual?

- Rituals happen when you are not present with the customer in other ways as well. What happens when they are home with your product? Can unwrapping it be a ritual? Can using it be a ritual? Can connecting with others about it on social media be a ritual? Can recycling the excess packaging be a ritual?

- What events can become rituals? Your annual summer sale? Your yearly employee barbecue? Your customer appreciation event? Your employee of the year announcement? Birthday cards to your customers? Special gifts to customers who have been with you for 20 years? Lapel pins awarded to people who have taken 10 tours with your company? To be a ritual these need to be done routinely. They must be dependable or they are not rituals.

- Think of several outrageous ideas for rituals. Let your mind wander to the quirky, the unusual, the goofy, the exotic. It must be authentic. It must be appropriate for your Meaningful Few. But most of us play it safe when it comes to new ideas. What can you come up with that is outside the safe zone?

What Are Your Rituals?

Stories

Why are we talking about stories?

Stories are a huge chunk of your branding because stories are communication. They can be the way to talk about our business, our beliefs, our customers, our products. They can entertain, but more importantly they can persuade. They can show a better future. They can inspire and delight. And stories are a way to offer proof.

Story is a word that has many definitions. So when talking about story we must be careful to explain which type of story we are talking about. We are talking about the purpose-told story.

Purpose-told stories are the foundation of your brand storytelling. These are stories that fit the classic story arc of introduction, trigger, conflict, climax, falling action, resolution. All of this can happen in a paragraph or across the 7 books of the Harry Potter series. As the author you get to decide who is your main character, how to make him someone we care about and what challenges and struggles he faces in order to reach his important goal.

In a business setting, your purpose stories might be why you founded this business, customer success stories, or leadership stories told to your employees. You might use stories of your customers as tools for overcoming objections to your product, pricing or other prospect concerns.

These purpose-told stories are a critical element of your branding.

Let your customer tell stories. Social media is wonderful for offering ways for customers to get in the act. Let them post on Facebook about using your product or results of your service. Let them post pictures on a Pinterest board or on Instagram. Encourage them to give details but don't worry about meeting the purpose-told story definition. These are in the anecdote story category and are very effective in creating engagement.

Reflections on Your Stories

- Do you already have stories that you use? How effective have they been?

- What is you founding story? Or a story about your passion for this business?

- What customer stories can you think of? Who needed something and tried other vendors without success until they found you? What is the story of their search?

- Think of objections to your product or service. Price, convenience, effectiveness, fear of change, or whatever. Can you create a story to explain why this isn't a valid objection? If you don't have a true story, then create a fictional one as an exercise. Is there a way this fictional story can become true?

- If you have done the beliefs, vision, and why me pages, you may have many thoughts you believe are valid. Do you have a story to support each one? If you don't why not? What do you need to do to prove the statement when you have no story?

- What stories do your customers have about your business? Do you celebrate those?

- Can you think of stories about your products or services and how they have changed someone's life?

- What stories can you tell about your company culture? Can you use these as recruiting tools? Or for introducing your culture to new employees?

- Can you add stories in unexpected places, like hang tags, package inserts, instruction labels, store signage, product descriptions, newspaper ads, new customer welcome packets?

- What stories can you use at networking events? Do you need stories for a funding pitch?

- What stories can you use on social media? And how can you get the customer involved?

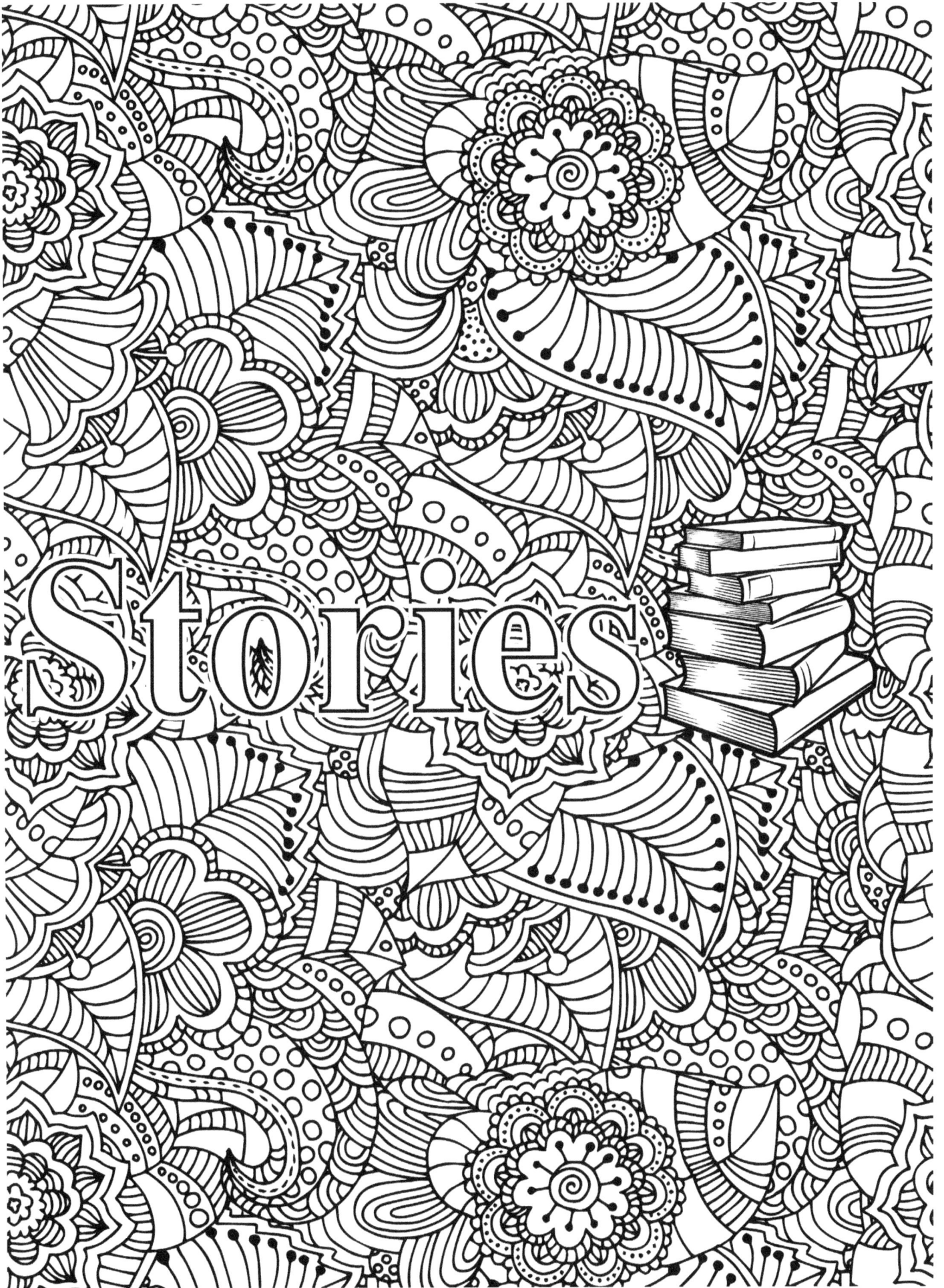

Stories

How Will You Use Stories?

Ecosystem

Why talk about a brand ecosystem? Because it is the perfect analogy for nurturing a brand and it works especially well for the small business owner or solopreneur.

An ecosystem is made of interconnected and interacting parts that work together. Going further with the ecosystem concept, we take an idea from the permaculture movement. Permaculture is a system of cultivation intended to maintain permanent agriculture or horticulture by relying on renewable resources and a self-sustaining ecosystem.

The four basic principles are:

1. Maximum result with minimum input. (Don't we all want that?)

2. Integration of all the elements. (All the parts combine to create a coordinated whole)

3. Synergy of all the elements. (All the parts support, enhance and leverage each other)

4. Sustainability. (Ignore trying to do it all. Ignore the latest social media fad. Focus on what you can do over the long haul.)

Your brand ecosystem will contain all the elements you have been thinking about: your beliefs, what you do, what you say, what you look like, your rituals, and your sensory elements.

These six drivers influence all your customer touch-points. This can be quite a few moving parts to coordinate! But since they are all working together it isn't as overwhelming as you may think.

Do you see how these permaculture definitions / principles can apply to branding? Producing the experience you want without depleting your resources? A permanent system. One that is self-sustaining. Repeatable efforts rather than time-consuming one-offs? That is how the tiniest business can have an Unstoppable Brand!

Reflections on Your Ecosystem

- A brand ecosystem is built in layers using your six brand drivers. Start with what you have now that fits with your desired brand feeling. Maybe you only have a logo and a tag line. That's OK.

- What brand elements do you think are needed and doable in the short term?

- What great brand ideas do you have that need more time or money than you have right now? Can you take a first step now? Or put this on your to do list for later?

- How do these elements support each other? Visual consistency is expected. Do they all promote your message? Does your web site encourage people to visit your Facebook page? Do your business cards promote your services?

- Do you repurpose elements? An interview becomes a podcast. A blog post becomes a SlideShare presentation, a workshop, then a speech? Multiple blog posts become an ebook?

- Do you carefully choose new technology and social media channels so you are only doing what you have time to do well and is right for your Meaningful Few?

- Do you have a variety of elements of varying impact? You web site might be your biggest branding element. But you should have small and medium size elements as well, such as business cards, ritual greetings, a signature fragrance, an annual clearance sale. Mix it up for greater effect.

- Do you have a checklist or process to make sure new brand elements are created with the consistency? What happens if you have new hires? How will they learn your brand strategy?

- What steps will you take to create a brand mindset? It won't continue on its own; you need to have concrete steps to nurture the habit. Now is a good time to identify those steps.

What Is Your Ecosystem?

Delight

What does it mean to delight a customer? This is really at the bottom of the branding question.

Delight means something that makes you very happy — something that gives you great pleasure or satisfaction. Isn't this what we want for our customers?

We have talked about the feeling you want to generate. We have talked about happiness for our customizers. So haven't we covered the topic of delight? Are we beating that dead horse here?

Not really. There is one more side to making people happy that we can reflect on. And that is the small things. The surprises. The unexpected.

People are funny. When looking at new houses, we are impressed with the chef-quality kitchen or the separate studio or the five bedrooms ready for us to occupy. These are big things that would be expensive (or impossible) to add later. But then we get attached to the little things.

We love the crown molding. in the dining room. Or the stained glass front door. Or the cute fence around the front yard.

These are things we could easily add on our own later. But their attraction is far stronger than they should be. These little things create an emotional pull for us, far outweighing their real value.

Think of your mother. She may have had many wonderful qualities. But when you look back at your youth you tend to remember the small moments. How she held your hand crossing the street. Or combed your hair for special occasions. Or brought your lunch to school when you forgot it. Or made your favorite chocolate chip cookies when you needed a lift.

So it goes with your customers. That old song was right: Little things do mean a lot.

Reflections on Delight

- Do you have little things in place now? What are they? Why do they delight your customers?

- Think about your Meaningful Few. What would surprise and delight them?

- Can you come up with a few experiments? Go back through all the ideas you have recorded while doing these pages. Where are there little things that you could try out? Put out special candies. Maybe have cupcakes on Tuesdays. Or include perfume samples with every order. If you are a local business what about partnering with another local business? Can you offer a small sample of their products as a surprise to yours?

- Maybe create relationships with several local businesses and switch up what you offer? A coupon for a free ice cream cone one week and a fresh tomato the next.

- People are delighted by exclusive experiences. Can you invite your loyal customers to a special evening of food drinks and entertainment? A fashion show? Or a tool demonstration? People love to see how things are made. Can you offer a behind-the-scenes look at one of your products?

- Delight also comes with sharing. What about bring-a-friend nights? Or family nights? May be you don't have a business suited to this, but you might partner with another business to offer a dinner, or roller skating party or hand massages.

- Hidden surprises are so fun. So rather than putting a coupon in the bag, why not hide it between the pages of the book or in the shoes they just purchased? Or a thank you note. Häagen Dazs ice cream knew that ice cream straight from the freezer was too cold and hard. Two minutes at room temperature resulted in the ideal consistency. So they created a two minute song that they put on iTunes. Under the lid of each ice cream container was a link to that song with instructions to download and listen while waiting for the ice cream to reach it's peak. The best part is this was a customer idea. What can you do for a fun experience? How are you collecting customer ideas?

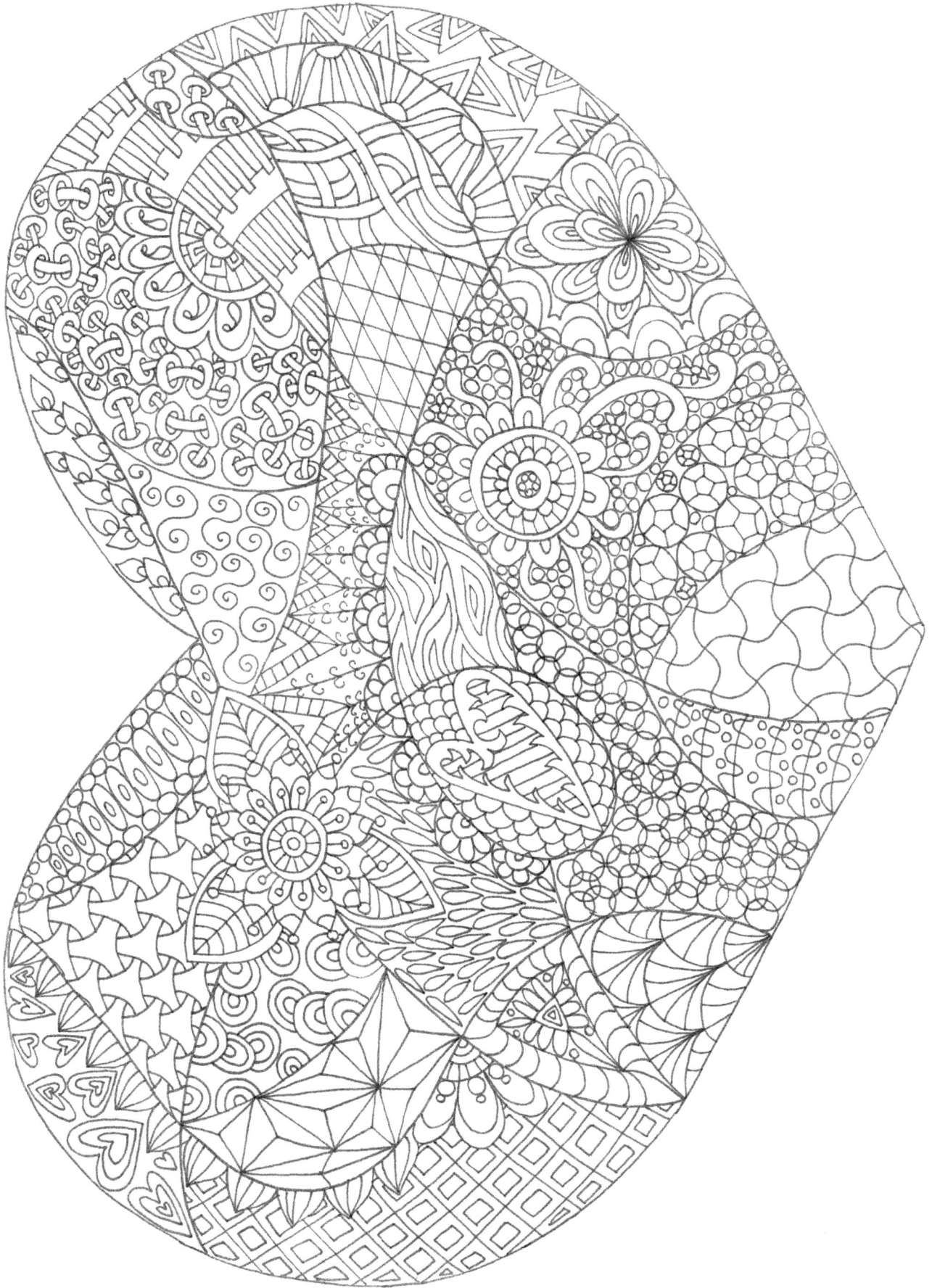

How Will You Delight People?

Your Topics

I hope you have found the coloring process valuable and fun.

In case you have other topics you would like to try, the following five coloring pages allow you to work on topics of your choice. Pricing? Staffing? Marketing tactics? Partnerships? Referral agents / supporters?

What are the worries that keep you up at night? The questions you don't have an answer for?

Identify the topic and then create your own questions for a guided reflection. The idea is to find those issues you are struggling with, or possibly avoiding because you don't know what to do. Let your stress-free brain and a coloring page help you discover the answers.

Don't forget:

Start where you are. Use what you have. Do what you can.

Best of luck with your new branding ideas!

Janet

Your Topic _____

Your Topic _____

Your Topic _____

Your Topic _____

Your Topic _____

Want More?

Visit www.unstoppablebrand.com for other resources.

Sign up for free email Story Sparks.

Enroll in a free 21 day branding mail course.

Get on my mailing list for future updates.

Or just send me a message, ask a question or provide feedback on this book.

Interested in marketing storytelling? Then you might enjoy my other book, *Your Unstoppable Brand: the practical guide to engaging your ideal customers through the power of stories*. It is available on Amazon.

To your branding success!

Janet

www.ingramcontent.com/pod-product-compliance
Lightning Source LLC
Chambersburg PA
CBHW051231200326
41519CB00025B/7330